Christmas in the Philippines

*This belen, or crèche, decorates St. Anthony
Parish Church in the province of Laguna.*

Christmas in the Philippines

**Christmas Around the World
From World Book**

World Book, Inc.
a Scott Fetzer company
Chicago

Christmas in the Philippines was prepared by the Editorial and Art Departments of World Book, Inc.

1996 Printing

Printed in Mexico.

ISBN: 0-7166-0890-1
Library of Congress Catalog Card No. 90-70099

The publisher wishes to thank the many individuals who took part in developing this publication.

Writer: Theresa Kryst Fertig
Consultants: Prudenciana C. Cruz and Monina A. Mercado

Special thanks go to Dr. Mary G. Acierto, Stan Bernal, Ramiro Cabrera, Lee Dutton, Tina Guerrero, Grace Mittenthal, Rosemary Mittenthal, Achilles H. Natividad, Soccoro Obaob, Perla Rigor, and Rosita Tan.

2 3 4 5 6 7 8 9 10 99 98 97 96

Contents

A Fitting Season

The Philippines is known as "the land of fiestas," and at Christmastime this is especially true. One of the first fiestas to take place in December is the Marian procession in honor of the Feast of the Immaculate Conception. The procession is a parade of images of the Virgin Mary from all over the Philippines. It takes place in Intramuros.

Christmas in the Philippines. Far across the ocean in this tropical island Asian nation, this very special occasion is more than a holiday. It is truly a national fiesta. Filipinos are proud to proclaim their Christmas celebration to be the longest and merriest in the world. It begins formally on December 16 with attendance at the first of nine pre-dawn Masses and continues nonstop until January 6, Three Kings Day, the official end of the season.

The Philippines, a land of ancient history, is the only Asian country where Christians predominate; the majority of its people are Roman Catholic. Christmas, therefore, is an extremely important and revered holiday for almost all Filipinos. As a people, they are very religious, and Christmas is especially meaningful for them. It is a time for family, for sharing, for giving, a time for food, fun, and friendship. In the Philippines, Christmas is celebrated, as best as can be, in the true spirit of the season.

Lying in the South China Sea a few hundred miles (kilometers) off the mainland of Asia, the Philippines includes more than 7,000 islands and covers an area of about 116,000 square miles (300,000 square kilometers). It is separated into three island groups: Luzon, to the north, is the largest island and is where the city of Manila is located; Mindanao, to the south, is the second largest island and is culturally very different in parts of the southeastern area which is home to most of the nation's Muslims; and the Visayas, in the middle, are a scattering of medium-sized islands. One glance at a map makes it easy to understand why the country's customs and traditions, as well as its people, are so diverse. Although English is widely used and is one of the country's official languages, Pilipino, based on the Tagalog dialect, is the national language. There are, however, about 35 different ethnic groups throughout the country and about 70 different dialects spoken in the Philippines.

Christianity, a very important part of Filipino culture, was brought to the Philippines by the Spanish colonizers in the 1500's. Ferdinand Magellan was the first explorer to "discover" this new land and claim it for Spain, though it was already inhabited by a people with a writing system, laws, and a culture of their own. They were of Malay origin and had arrived from Indonesia and Malaysia thousands of years earlier. The Spanish missionaries, however, were very effective in converting these people to Christianity, thus maintaining a stronghold that would last for centuries.

Many vestiges reminiscent of that early colonization and religious background remain throughout the Philippines, all held in high honor and esteem by Filipinos. A cross stands in the nation's oldest city, Cebu City, which is located on the island of Cebu in the Visayas. This cross encases fragments of the original cross believed to have been planted by Magellan and his crew when they heard Mass to celebrate their safe arrival. And Cebu's San Agustin Church, the oldest in the nation, houses Cebu's most prized possession: the Santo Niño de Cebu. The Santo Niño (Holy Child) is a hand-carved, wooden image of the infant Jesus, richly clad in elegant robes. It is said to have been presented as a baptismal gift by Magellan to the wife of the Cebu chieftain in 1521.

In Manila, the most imposing Spanish relic is Intramuros, the old walled city of Manila, which was begun in 1571. A thick ancient wall still surrounds the city and its old cobblestone streets. Within the walls were once situated important buildings, the houses of

Devotees gather and kneel around the Santo Niño de Cebu (Holy Child of Cebu) in Cebu's San Agustin Church.

feudal lords, and about a dozen or more churches. Nearly all of this was leveled, however, during the World War II Battle of Manila when American forces liberated the city in 1945 from the Japanese. Incredibly, the only structure left standing completely intact in Intramuros after the war was Manila's San Agustin Church, built in 1599. It contains the tombs of several Spanish *conquistadores* (conquerors), numerous antiquities, remarkable wood carvings, and a beautiful trompe-l'oeil ceiling.

This venerable old church has survived not only wars, but fires and earthquakes as well. It has been said of San Agustin's that "its tranquility belies its past." Christmas Mass here is a remarkable experience. The rest of Intramuros has been restored where possible and when not, modern buildings have been reconstructed following the Spanish colonial architectural style.

Spanish influence in the Philippines is indeed profound, not only in the nation's religious beliefs and Christmas customs, but in many aspects of Filipino culture. It was the Spanish who gave this island country its name (in honor of the crown prince who would eventually become King Philip II of Spain) and who ruled it for more than 300 years. Certainly Christmas in the Philippines has many ties to that early Spanish background.

This is not to say that Spanish is the only influence evident in the Philippines today. Indians, Spanish, Chinese, British, Americans, and Japanese have all come to the islands, each group leaving its mark—on such things as foods, clothing,

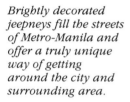

Brightly decorated jeepneys fill the streets of Metro-Manila and offer a truly unique way of getting around the city and surrounding area.

More than 7,000 islands covering about 116,000 square miles (300,000 square kilometers) make up the Philippines. It's no wonder it is a land of such diverse people and customs.

The church is the main focus of Christmas in the Philippines. This old church outside Manila is decorated with parols, *or star lanterns, for the season.*

language, and a variety of other customs. In total, a unique, colorful evolution has occurred in the Philippines with one culture overlaid upon another, each still gripping to the Filipino's basic personality, creating a diverse group of very special people with very special customs and traditions.

Thus Christmas, though celebrated throughout the Philippines with universal fervor, can vary in its customs from province to province. One might hear Christmas carols gloriously sung in one of the major languages, such as English, Pilipino, or Cebuano.

What might be a Christmas tradition for one family or community on the island of Leyte in the eastern Visayas might be an unfamiliar oddity among the pine forests in Baguio City, a mountain resort north of Manila. A traditional community pageant celebrating the Nativity in Cavite may be unknown in Cebu.

Christmas in the Philippines is certainly a mixture of Western and native Filipino tradition. Santa Claus, the Christmas tree, sending Christmas cards, and singing Christmas carols have all been inherited from the cultures of the West. They have, however, been well adapted to fit the nature and personality of the people. It is indeed the people that remain an unfluctuating constant in the Filipino Christmas celebration—their gracious nature, their incredible hospitality, their devotion to their religious faith, and their immense respect for family and friends, particularly their elders.

To most Filipinos, family and friends are the greatest source of strength. Their families are large. They tend to have many children, and often three generations live together. They love to share their homes with relatives, friends, even strangers. Filipinos are naturally warm-hearted and generous.

Some say it is inbred, learned in childhood and passed from generation to generation. There is an old Malay proverb that may well explain this Filipino characteristic:

**A debt of gold
can be repaid.
A debt of hospitality
you carry to the grave.**

Thus their homes are always open; their tables are always full. Nothing is too much trouble to make a guest feel welcome. No season or occasion reflects this indescribable hospitality more than Christmas.

There is no snow in the Philippines at Christmastime. There are very few pine trees.

Even without snow or pine trees, there's no doubt it's Christmas in the Philippines. Filipino Christmas decorations are abundant and beautiful.

There is no traditional Yule log or fetching of the pine sprigs from the woods. Santa Claus, though visible in displays and known to exist by Filipino children, very seldom comes bearing gifts. But no matter! Filipinos have their own unique traditions that make Christmas special for them. The bamboo *parol* (pah ROLE), or star lantern, is *the* symbol of Christmas in the Philippines, representing the guiding light, the star of Bethlehem. It emits a warmth unparalleled among holiday adornments and is unique to the Philippines. In no other country is this lighted star used as widely and as aptly as a Christmas decoration.

*F*ilipinos decorate everywhere for the season with enthusiasm. From the big, bustling cities to the impoverished rural areas, nothing goes unadorned. Even the ever-present jeepneys in Metro-Manila will be decorated for the holidays. Jeepneys originated from the army surplus jeeps left behind by Americans after World War II. Today, these "pop art" taxi-buses are made to resemble those old army jeeps. Jeepneys are always painted bright colors and covered with stickers, streamers, and other fancy accessories. But at Christmastime they are especially bedecked. Strings of tiny lights, the traditional

parol, or even a small manger scene may adorn the jeepneys. And, of course, Christmas music blares from the portable stereo radio for all to enjoy. In the rural *barrios*, or villages, though holiday embellishments are not nearly so elaborate, residents still believe that even the most humble home must be trimmed with the star lantern for Christmas.

But for Christian Filipinos, the focus of the Christmas celebration remains the church. Nearly every town has a Roman Catholic church, for about 85 per cent of all Filipinos are Catholic, and church holidays are well observed. The Catholic religion in the Philippines is marked by numerous colorful fiestas, which have evolved from years of Spanish rule and are often patterned after similar rituals in Latin America and Europe. Fiestas are an important part of Filipino life, a combination of religious symbolism and social life. They have both a spiritual and folk background, further evidence of the remarkable ability of the Filipino people to assimilate and cling to all of their past cultural influences.

Consequently, the Philippines has been called "the land of fiestas." Every town or barrio puts on its own fiesta at least once a year, usually to commemorate the feast day of its patron saint. There are colorful processions, large family and community gatherings,

Flowers are an appropriate decoration any time of year in the Philippines. But at Christmastime, they are especially popular. These vendors are ready with a good supply.

and always great quantities of food. Though it has been suggested in the past that fiestas be banned in favor of a less elaborate and more productive use of money and energy, Filipinos would not hear of it, refusing to relinquish this cherished tradition.

To most Filipinos, Christmas is the most anticipated fiesta of the year and is celebrated accordingly. The splendid climate of this tropical island nation, the abundance and beauty of its fresh flowers and lovely landscape, its multitude of culinary delights, and above all its warm-hearted people with their true devotion to family and faith all contribute to a holiday cele-

brated in the true Philippine fiesta tradition.

There is a word in the Pilipino language—*Mabuhay* (mah BOO hy)—that is used to say "Hello," "Cheers!" or, most often, "Welcome to the Philippines!" However, its literal translation is "May you live" or "Live life to the full." How fitting a word to welcome visitors to a land of warm climate, warm people, and the warmest of celebrations— Christmas in the Philippines! And so, to all, Mabuhay! and *Maligayang Pasko!* (mah lee gah YANG PAHS koh)—Merry Christmas Philippine style!

The Season Begins

December 16 is the true beginning of the Christmas season in the Philippines. Of course holiday wares have been placed for sale, and brightly colored decorations have been visible in shops throughout Philippine towns and cities long before this date. And the melodious strains of Christmas carols can be heard before November comes to a close. It is, however, December 16 that actually marks the official commencement of the Christmas holiday. Filipinos truly consider their Christmas festivities to be the longest and liveliest in the world.

It is on December 16 that most all Filipinos are awakened well before dawn by the tolling of the church bells calling them to the first *Misa de Gallo* (MEE suh deh GAHL yoh). *Misa de Gallo* is a Spanish term and translated means "Mass of the Rooster" since it is celebrated very early in the morning, 4 o'clock to be exact, at the first cockcrow. For nine mornings until Christmas Eve, the faithful arise

Fresh pine trees are too expensive for many Filipinos. Most families opt for handmade trees, which can be any shape, size, or color!

before dawn and attend Mass as a novena, a Catholic term for nine days of prayer. These nine days' devotion prior to Christmas is now called *Simbang Gabi* (sihm bahng gah BEE) by most Filipinos, a Tagalog term meaning "Night Mass." Simbang Gabi culminates on Christmas Eve with Midnight Mass, which may be referred to as Misa de Gallo, but is most likely called *Misa de Aguinaldo*. The terms are sometimes used interchangeably. Misa de Aguinaldo, meaning "Gift Mass," alludes to the gifts offered to the Christ child by the shepherds.

Simbang Gabi was first celebrated in the early 1700's as a Mass of thanksgiving for a fruitful harvest and to pray for a favorable year ahead. To be practical, the celebration was arranged to coincide with Christmas and *Noche Buena* (NOH chay BWAY nuh), the great feasting that occurs on Christmas Eve. The custom became so well accepted and successful that it spread far and wide and eventually evolved into the present-day celebration of Simbang Gabi.

Some say these predawn Masses are held at such an early hour as a form of necessary sacrifice; others contend the hour was an accommodation for the farmers who wanted to be working in their fields at the crack of dawn. Both may well be true. Whatever the case, today most Filipinos feel strongly that they haven't celebrated Christmas properly unless they have attended Simbang Gabi. This early morning sacrifice for them plays an important part in the commemoration of Christmas.

Beginning on the 16th in rural areas, villagers are often awakened by the sounds of firecrackers or handmade bamboo cannons (usually popular for New Year's Eve revelry) in the early mornings. Or the town band might traverse the village an hour before Mass playing a variety of carols to awaken the residents. Barefoot children, those who enjoy arising early, often follow close behind the musicians, stepping in time to the music all the way to the churchyard. In very small communities, the parish priest may himself knock on every door calling the faithful to Mass. Today, very often Christmas carols are sung or played over the church loudspeakers prior to Mass to awaken the townspeople.

The family attends Mass together, children as well as adults. Although some families feel the hour is too early for the children and think it best that little ones get their rest, many others believe it is as important for children to attend the predawn Masses as for adults, drowsy or not. Occasionally a gentle pinch is administered during the service if small heads tend to nod or tiny mouths open

Hundreds of parish-ioners gather to cele-brate the predawn mass of Simbang Gabi *at Las Piñas Church.*

wide in a yawn. But for all, the sleepiness eventually gives way to the beauty of the occasion. The smooth tones of the choir voices in song accompanied by the majestic organ and the beautiful sound of flutes, violins, and guitars ensure that by the end of Mass every worshiper is wide awake. For nine consecutive mornings, in the cool darkness of December, the churches are full—with people, with song, with prayer, with spirit. Christmas has truly begun!

But if Filipinos attend Simbang Gabi with great religious devotion, so do they look forward equally enthusiastically to the socializing that occurs after each Mass outside the church.

For it is here on the church plaza that numerous food stalls and carts appear lining the churchyard and the surrounding streets—another sign that Christmas has definitely arrived. Vendors with earthen ovens sell the delicious Philippine delicacies that churchgoers are anxious to purchase as an early breakfast treat. The hourlong liturgy at such an early hour, not to mention the wonderfully sweet aroma that has been floating through the air, has left most parishioners with a genuinely peaked appetite. And to gather and chat with friends just as the sun's first rays are peeking over the horizon is an especially enjoyable experience following

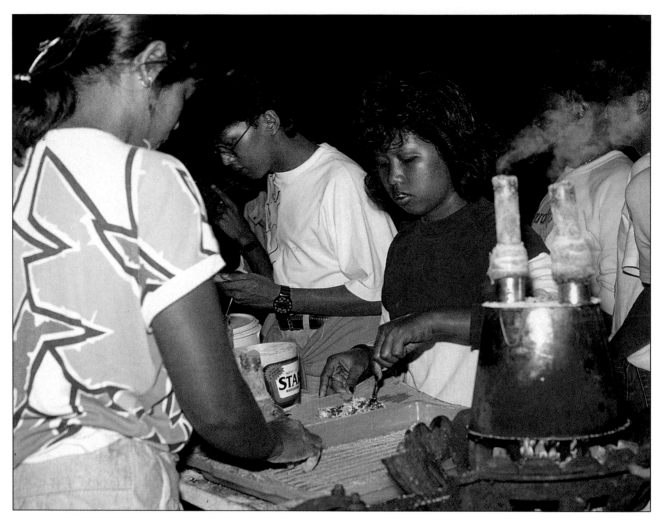

In the churchyard, vendors prepare puto bumbong, *a type of rice cake, for the hungry parishioners who will soon be coming from* Simbang Gabi.

an inspiring Christmas Mass.

Lines form to buy such specialties as *puto bumbong,* a rice cake made with a bluish-purple, sticky rice steamed in a cylindrical bamboo mold. The cake is tapped out and served with a sprinkling of brown sugar and shredded coconut meat. *Bibingka* is another mouth-watering treat whose sweet fragrance filters through the cool December air. This also is a type of rice cake. A popular version of bibingka is made with rice flour, eggs, and milk; baked; and topped with cheese, grated coconut, and salted eggs. *Suman,* another favorite, is a mixture of sticky rice, coconut milk, and sugar wrapped in banana or palm leaves and boiled or steamed. All of these, of course, are served with steaming hot *salabat,* a tealike drink made with ginger; or a rich, thick, hot chocolate known as *tsokolate.* Both are favorite drinks any time of year among Filipinos.

Once such goodies have been purchased, churchgoers have several options. Some hurry home to enjoy their warm breakfast delights in their own kitchens. Others may choose to take their refreshments as they leisurely stroll home socializing with friends and neighbors as the first light of dawn is just beginning to color the streets. Many people like to buy extra treats to take home for a "second" breakfast later in the morning. Or perhaps those who can't afford such a luxury or prefer their own homemade varieties will visit with friends awhile and then hurry home to their waiting delicacies.

This is a special time during the Christmas holidays for all Filipinos. Everyone looks forward to Simbang Gabi and the social time afterward that goes with it. In fact, some will secretly admit that these early-morning, seemingly chance meetings, complete with culinary treats, are the reward for getting up so early.

Christmas caroling is a favorite holiday activity among Filipinos. Though a Western custom, it has been adopted with incredible enthusiasm throughout the Philippines. On the first day of Simbang Gabi, groups of carolers become abundant everywhere, in rural villages as well as big cities.

Christmas shoppers have a hard time choosing that perfect gift.

Some, usually youngsters unable to restrain their zeal, begin earlier. Each night, beginning December 16, from 6 o'clock in the evening until nearly midnight, the sounds of familiar carols continually fill the air. Groups with a varied makeup—very young children, teen-agers, even adults—roam the village streets singing out the lovely Filipino carols they love so much, as well as English tunes they have come to know.

"Ang Pasko Ay Sumapit" ("Christmas Has Come"), is a traditional Filipino carol frequently sung during the holiday season by young and old alike. Often there are Pilipino translations of familiar English carols or beautiful native carols in the Tagalog or Cebuano languages. Among the best-loved and most frequently heard English carols are "Jingle Bells" and, interestingly, "White Christmas." The latter, of course, is something of which most Filipinos know nothing about. A "white Christmas" in the Philippines is just about impossible.

These nightly carolers in the Philippines might be members of a civic organization trying to raise needed funds. Perhaps they belong to a church group out for an evening of holiday socializing. They might be simply a group of neighborhood youngsters interested in making a little money. For as the carol-ers make the rounds of the village, they are greeted by residents who offer them a treat of candy or food or possibly a few *centavos* for their savings. Then again, there are those who carol simply for the fun of it; they enjoy being out and about during the holidays singing and enjoying the Philippine Christmas spirit.

In some regions of the Philippines the custom of caroling is elaborated somewhat with a ritual of Spanish or Mexican origin that truly enlivens the Christmas season. Groups of carolers called *pastores* (pah STAWR ays), or shepherds, make the rounds of their neighborhoods going from door to door. They are colorfully costumed in native folk outfits and accompanied by musicians playing guitars and castanets. These young men and women perform a traditional ring dance and serenade the townsfolk with Christmas carols, ballads, love songs, and native folk melodies. Frequently, the troupe will reenact scenes from the Nativity story with individuals taking the parts of Mary and Joseph and other Gospel characters. The villagers often reward the group with donations of money or food. A community might even prepare ahead for the performance by providing a special area and proper lighting for the production. Everyone gathers together in the street to enjoy the show. The village children love to join in and follow the vividly attired pastores as they travel the neighborhood beginning each afternoon and continuing well into the night during the nine days prior to Christmas.

The one element of Christmas, however, that truly symbolizes the Yuletide season for all Filipinos is the parol. On December 16, these beautiful, handcrafted, star-shaped lanterns appear everywhere—decorating homes, churches, schools, stores, city streets, even jeepneys. They are fashioned with bamboo sticks, covered with brightly colored rice paper or cellophane, and usually feature a tassel, maybe even one at each point. No Filipino home is too poor to have a parol. Families hang one in nearly every window and often use them to adorn the outside yard as well. Traditionally, a candle placed inside the lantern would be carefully lit each night of the season. With the advent of electricity, however, an electric light bulb is a more common alternative. These lanterns come in a variety of sizes and ingenious designs. But the most popular shape, by far, is the star. It represents the star of Bethlehem. The parol is indeed *the* sign of Christmas in the Philippines.

Families might purchase their lanterns in stores or from the many vendors who sell these festive decorations early in December along nearly every city street. Rural roadways, too, become scattered with stalls peddling lanterns. A lantern-making family might set up a shop right outside their home. One can often catch a glimpse of artisans at work on their parols alongside those displayed for sale. It's a difficult decision, selecting just the right lantern. Many Filipino families choose to make their own lanterns, particularly in rural areas. Rare is the barrio dweller who knows not how to make a parol, though it is a somewhat complicated process. Most Filipinos learn how to do it in school, where parol making is a traditional art project. Of course each lantern is carefully wrapped after the holiday is over and tucked safely away for next year. New ones will be made or purchased next December, however, since these are fragile ornaments and a few always manage to be destroyed in the packing and storing process.

Filipinos enjoy decorating their homes, not only with the star lanterns, but with all sorts of Christmas decorations. Brightly colored buntings or streamers are hung inside and out. Often Christmas cards, which are very beautiful and illustrate scenes of the Philippines, are pinned to red and green ribbons. The cards are then hung in the *sala,* or living room, for all to enjoy. Candles and wreaths are also common adornments. Recently, some Fil-

The parol, *or star lantern, is an essential Christmas decoration in the Philippines. This artisan is wiring a lantern so it will become a dazzling display of light and color.*

ipinos have begun choosing wreaths and other decorations made with local native materials rather than those patterned after Western designs. And many houses, particularly those in urban areas, are strung with tiny multicolored lights, both inside and out. Almost all Filipinos feel decorating their homes for the holidays is a must.

The Christmas tree is a Western custom that has been adopted and adapted to the Philippine life style. It is a decoration that almost no Filipino home is without. Perhaps it will be set up in the living area or, better yet, on the outside porch so that everyone in the village can enjoy its beauty. For those families who choose to buy a fresh pine tree, there are usually some for sale in various regions of the Philippines. These trees have been transported by truck or train from the lush pine forests of Baguio City, north of Manila. But these are generally very expensive. Artificial trees are more often the rule. Should a family decide against a real or artificial Christmas tree, there

are alternatives. Filipinos can be extremely creative in making a Christmas tree. Often a palm branch from a tree in the back-yard will suffice. Placed in a stand and decorated, it makes a perfect Christmas tree. Other families might make a tree out of triangular-shaped pieces of card-board put together in a three-dimensional form. Bare twigs, too, are nailed to a stand to make a perfectly symmetrical cone-shaped tree that is spray-painted in silver or gold, white or green.

Decorations for the tree might consist of tiny star lanterns, candies or fruits tied with ribbons, small wood or bamboo carvings, shells painted bright colors, little baskets, ornaments made of colored rice paper, tinsel icicles or other glittery items, and empty matchboxes wrapped as presents. Some Filipinos may remember years back making artificial snow to place on the tree to imitate a cold-weather climate. Old soap pieces would be collected, boiled down in a pot, and then beaten, sometimes for hours, until just the right frothy consistency. This mixture would be placed on the branches of the tree and allowed to dry and harden. Cotton balls or crumpled rice paper were also used to simulate snow. What fun to have a snow-covered Christmas tree in the house! Today, however, Filipinos feel this is unrealistic, and generally shy away from imitation snow on their Christmas trees.

City streets and village buildings are decorated for the holidays as well. Some of the elegant shopping districts in Metro-Manila, which includes the city of Manila and all of its surrounding suburbs, are aglitter with a myriad of lights and other holiday decorations—truly a sight to see at this time of year. Gold or silver fringed buntings or brightly colored garlands are draped high above city streets. Lanterns can be seen dangling from street lamps and in store windows enticing shoppers to come in and buy the wonderful Christmas wares—candles, tinsel, wreaths, stars, or sweet treats and candies. Who can resist? Occasionally artificial snow and even Santa Claus are part of the display—signs of the Western influence on Christmas in the Philippines. And the Manila COD Department Store, in Quezon City, erects a fabulous mechanical Christmas display outside the store each year that attracts numerous onlookers during the holiday season. A different theme is depicted every year, perhaps Santa in a rocket ship or the Three Kings in a jet plane. It is said that as soon as the display is dismantled after the holiday is over, plans begin for next year's exhibit.

Often public squares or large commercial areas have a giant Christmas tree aglow with holiday decorations for all to enjoy. Roxas Boulevard, a major thoroughfare in Manila, is festively illuminated with lanterns and lights. The Cultural Center of the Philippines, located on this famous boulevard, annually displays a giant radiant lantern on its facade. And all the trees, shrubs, and plants in the plaza in Makati, a Metro-Manila suburb, are beautifully decorated for the season with glimmering lights.

The Malacañang Palace, a special attraction in the Manila area any time of year, is particularly lovely at Christmas. The palace is located in a tropical setting on the bank of the winding Pasig River in San Miguel, Manila. It was built by a Spanish aristocrat, and its name is derived from Tagalog words. Fishermen would sail past and say *"May lakan diyan"*—"A nobleman lives there." It used to be the official residence of Philippine presidents. But since

Each year, the Manila COD Department Store builds a mechanical Christmas display for the shoppers' enjoyment.

the election of President Cora-zon Aquino, the gardens and executive building of the palace have been opened to the public and now house a historical museum. The president continues to govern from the palace guesthouse but lives elsewhere. At Christmastime the beautiful white palace is strung with lights and lanterns. Here, sometime during the week before Christmas, the government's cabinet members and their families join the president's family to have dinner and sing Christmas carols. There is also a gathering for children at the palace during the week preceding Christmas. The spouses of cabinet members and perhaps the president will greet needy youngsters and present them with gifts that have been collected from citizens so that all children of the Metro-Manila area might have a merry Christmas. The president's gift-giving program extends to the provinces as well. Gifts and toys are parceled and sent to depressed areas all over the Philippines to be distributed by military personnel or social workers to needy children.

The nation's churches, both Roman Catholic and those of the Philippine Independent Church, an offshoot of the Roman Catholic Church, are especially trimmed for the holidays by church members. Large lanterns are hung on each pillar inside the church as well as from tree branches in the churchyard. Small white or multicolored lights might delicately outline the outside perimeter of the church building. Inside, the altar is festooned with fragrant fresh flowers, such as the sampaguita, a white, star-shaped flower with a lovely jasminelike scent; it's the national flower of the Philippines. And at the side altar is the most significant component of the church's Christmas celebration—the *belen,* or Nativity scene.

Belen (beh LEHN) is the Spanish word for Bethlehem and has come to name the tableau that represents the Nativity scene. It is the oldest symbol of Philippine Christmas. It traveled originally from Italy, where Saint Francis of Assisi created the first Nativity scene with live donkeys and oxen, to Spain, then to Mexico, finally arriving in the Philippines during the 1700's. Traditionally, the place for the belen was in the church. The first ones were very ornate, often life-sized. The scene included both common and divine characters—shepherds and peasants mingling with kings and angels—all in awe of the infant in the manger. In most churches, the belen is prepared by December 16, before the first predawn Mass of Simbang Gabi. Of course, the Holy Infant is absent from the belen and does not appear until Midnight Mass on Christmas Eve. Some churches

Christmas trees decorate many public places during the holidays. This tree, made of lights, illuminates the area near Manila's international airport.

in the Philippines might have a second belen on display outside the church, perhaps on the lawn in a grotto setting or in the church plaza.

Gradually, the belen made its way from the church into Filipino homes. Though much smaller, each home belen is just as elaborately arranged and positioned in a place of honor, perhaps under the Christmas tree or in some other special spot. It is usually Mother who has the distinction of arranging the figures of Mary, Joseph, the shepherds, the cattle and other animals, and the Three Kings in their proper places. Over the years the typical Filipino belen has appeared in a variety of versions from the folk-art look to very modern designs. It might be made of wood, ivory, porcelain, plaster, stone, ceramic, metal, fiber, or even paper. However elaborate or simple, each holds a special place in the hearts and homes of all Filipinos. Some families even keep a belen on display in their home all year around.

But the belen is no longer confined to church and home. It has found its way all across Philippine towns and villages, into public parks, shopping malls, department stores, and movie house lobbies. Even jeepneys may have a belen added to their other holiday adornments. The local police station might display a belen in its window or outside its door. Many Philippine villages set up a belen in the town plaza, similar to our custom of displaying a large community Christmas tree. And the Malacañang Palace has usually had two belens set out, one in front of the executive building and another in front of the president's quarters. This tableau commemorating the birth of Christ establishes the religious meaning of Christmas, its basic appeal to the people of the Philippines. It is an affirmation of the people's religious faith.

These weeks before Christmas are very busy ones in the Philippines. Everyone is concerned with preparing and decorating. Children are particularly eager and engrossed at this time of year. Though most Philippine schools are closed for a week or two during the Christmas holiday, there is a great deal of activity that goes on at school in the weeks before vacation begins. Pageants, programs, and parties are all part of the school celebration. Often schoolchildren, directed by an able and enthusiastic teacher, will present a reenactment of the Nativity. Each child has a part. Some are donkeys, sheep, or goats; others are kings, shepherds, or angels; and the lucky ones get the parts of Mary and Joseph. Families come from near and far; all the neighboring barrios are invited. These pageants are often held in the outdoor auditoriums of schools or churches since the weather is usually pleasant. Christmas carols are always a part of the program, with everyone singing along.

Parol making is another school Christmas activity Filipino children look forward to. They take much pride in these Christmas parols, carefully transporting them home to hang in the window. There may be a school lantern parade as a culmination of the holiday activities. Perhaps a competition will be held with judges awarding the best efforts in lantern making. Each classroom joins in the parade and follows with a Christmas party and a gift exchange as the

The belen, *or crèche, decorates many public places in the Philippines at Christmastime. This life-sized* belen *is in front of an office building in Makati, Metro-Manila's financial district.*

classmates bid "Maligayang Pasko!" to one another until school resumes in January.

Businesses, offices, and other workplaces are buzzing as well with holiday excitement. There are office parties and gift exchanges or grab bags, because giving and sharing is a very important part of Christmas for all Filipinos. Employees often receive a Christmas bonus of some sort from their employers, usually money. And everyone has a day or two off at Christmas—it's a national holiday. Some workers arrange to take additional vacation days at Christmastime because they are expecting many visitors during these festive weeks; all must be ready. There is cooking to be done, cleaning to arrange, food to be purchased, and new clothing to be bought or sewed. The season has indeed begun!

The Long Night Before Christmas

C hristmas Eve in the Philippines is a long-awaited night. For some, it is a night without sleep, a continuous celebration moving right into Christmas Day. As December 24 dawns, the last Mass of Simbang Gabi is attended; then preparations begin for Noche Buena. Noche Buena is the family feast that takes place following Midnight Mass on Christmas Eve.

By the time Christmas Eve arrives, much has already been done to prepare for the special day. Many Filipinos think of this celebration of the birth of Christ as a time of rebirth or renewal. The house must be thoroughly cleaned. New items for the household might be purchased to replace old or worn-out things. Filipinos prepare their homes not only for the arrival of family members and friends for the holiday, but also for a very special visitor— Jesus is coming.

New clothes are a must. One cannot attend Mass Christmas morning without something new

A family gathers by the tree to celebrate Christmas. Gifts are exchanged, prayers are said, and carols are sung.

The open markets all over Metro-Manila, including the Quinta market, are busy with shoppers who are preparing for the Noche Buena *feast.* Noche Buena *takes place after Midnight Mass on Christmas Eve.*

and festive for the occasion. The boys invariably need new pants, the girls new dresses, and everyone needs new shoes. Perhaps mothers or grandmothers with a talent for sewing make these necessary articles of clothing. If not, such items can be purchased at a local market or department store.

And so, homes and families throughout the Philippines are properly prepared. The local church and churchyard, too, are carefully cleaned to be ready for the appearance of the Holy Infant in the belen on Christmas Eve. And it is important to most Filipinos at this time to prepare and cleanse their souls as well. Many are sure to go to confession at their parish church just prior to Christmas Eve.

In the days and weeks before Christmas Eve, kitchens are abundantly stocked with

necessary food items. It is extremely important to have enough food for Noche Buena and the remaining days of the holiday. Some families save all year so that their Christmas table will be properly filled. Some may even borrow in order to celebrate in what they feel is the appropriate manner.

Thus, the markets all across this island nation are filled with busy shoppers during the month of December. Beginning the last week in November until after New Year's Day, Filipinos flock to large open markets such as the Quinta market in a district in downtown Manila where they can purchase fresh fruits and vegetables; fresh meats, poultry, and fish; cheeses; flowers—any of the items to make the Noche Buena feast perfect. Hawkers sell their wares in stalls set up along the sidewalks near the Quinta market. During the Christmas season they carry Christmas decorations of all kinds, firecrackers for New Year's noisemaking, or anything else one might want or need for the holidays. The sidewalks are virtually impassable. Divisoria is another large marketplace in Manila where Filipinos can purchase the dry goods they may need for Christmas—tablecloths, curtains, fabrics, wreaths, bells, or any variety of Christmas decorations—all sold at wholesale prices. And Baclaran, an open air market in the southern area of Metro-Manila, is frequented by Filipinos who come from farther south in Luzon. Here one can find all the important foods, canned goods, or dry goods required for the holiday celebration. Markets, not only in urban areas but in towns and villages throughout the provinces, are teeming with goods and people.

Back home in the kitchen on Christmas Eve morning, the lus-

In some areas of the Philippines, a panunuluyan—a *reenactment of the Nativity story—precedes the celebration of Midnight Mass.*

cious aromas of a multitude of specialty foods being prepared for Noche Buena mingle and sift through the air as final preparations are completed elsewhere in the house. Colorful streamers are hung, last-minute decorations are placed on the tree, baskets of fresh fruits are prepared, packages are wrapped, or some fresh flowers are brought in to scent the house with their beautiful fragrance. And finally, children might be coaxed into taking a short nap so that they will be ready for the inevitable late-night celebrating.

Often by 10 o'clock, churches are filled with people waiting to celebrate Midnight Mass. No one wants to miss this glorious occasion.

For some Filipinos the Christmas Eve gathering begins early in the evening so that all family members can congregate and attend Midnight Mass together. The evening may be hosted by Grandmother and Grandfather, or perhaps by an aunt or uncle with the biggest house. Often the family member who can most afford the Noche Buena feast agrees to host the celebration. But wherever the merrymaking takes place, it is not limited to family members alone. Anyone is welcome. Some may bring relatives from their

*Because of the crowds, not everyone
gets a seat at Midnight Mass.*

spouse's side of the family. Or they may bring friends. And all neighbors are welcome. The more the merrier!

Often, around 8 o'clock, groups of serenaders dressed in colorful costumes appear on the streets singing Christmas carols with guitars and banjos. Christmas Eve, before Midnight Mass, is a favorite time for caroling. Family members might carol together, stopping at the homes of other relatives or friends, and then all continue on to Midnight Mass.

The church is filled very early for Midnight Mass, often by 10 o'clock. Frequently the crowd overflows onto the church patio. Carols are sung before Mass begins. Parishioners dressed in their very best clothes gather together to celebrate this special Mass. Some Filipinos feel new Christmas garments cannot be worn until they have first been worn to church, either to Midnight Mass or to Mass on Christmas morning. The children, of course, are eager to dress up and proudly display their new apparel.

*I*n some provinces of the Philippines, such as Cavite and Bulacan, a festivallike production called a *panunuluyan* (pan oo noo LOO yahn) is held on Christmas Eve before Midnight Mass. The weary flight of Mary and Joseph as they search for shelter is reenacted by costumed townsfolk as a sort of pastoral pageant or street theater. The panunuluyan can be one of two versions; one uses live players to take the parts of Mary and Joseph, while the other uses statues of the Holy Couple with singers vocalizing each part. In either case, the group sets out into the streets of the village, perhaps around 9 o'clock, accompanied by candle-bearers, a brass band, the church choir, and many villagers. They go from house to house, and at each door the Holy Couple sings out its plea for shelter. Each homeowner, representing an innkeeper, replies in song informing the Couple that the inns are already filled to capacity. The search and pageant finally end in the church at about the stroke of midnight, where the entire panunuluyan cast assembles near the altar in a Nativity scene, just in time to celebrate for Midnight Mass.

In most churches throughout the Philippines, it is during the celebration of Midnight Mass that the Infant Jesus is lowered into the belen, or Nativity scene, often with a shower of flowers, tolling church bells, and choir voices raised in song. After Mass, which can last for over an hour, the belen is open so that the mesmerized congregation may greet the newborn child.

When Mass is over, already in the early hours of the morning, everyone is ready for the fun to begin. Some families or groups of friends may go caroling. With one or two guitar-playing members, the group proceeds through the village to the homes of friends or relatives merrily singing carols. After enjoying some scrumptious treats offered to them at homes here and there, they finally arrive at their own Noche Buena where at least one member of the family has stayed behind to attend to last-minute preparations or to remain with the children. Often the younger children do not attend Midnight Mass because of the hour. Those who stayed behind will attend Mass on Christmas morning.

As everyone begins arriving home after Midnight Mass, the little ones are awakened from their naps—if, that is, they were able to overcome their excitement enough to fall asleep in the first place. The food is brought out and the festivities begin.

The table is set buffet style with as many as 15 to 20 food items that are constantly replenished when a dish runs low. *Arroz caldo,* a chicken and rice soup, is a typical dish on the Noche Buena table. Another is *lumpia,* a spring roll filled with a mixture of any meat, fish, or vegetable combination in a wrapper made of flour and water. *Pancit* is a noodle dish served quite often in the Philippines. It can be prepared in a variety of ways,

After Midnight Mass, carolers spread warmth and joy to neighbors.

but often with pork or chicken, cabbage, and celery. *Rellenong manok,* boned stuffed chicken, is truly fiesta fare. The chicken is boned, roasted, and stuffed with ham, pork, sausage, and pickles, and then sliced and served. It is a culinary masterpiece and is displayed with great pride. Similarly *rellenong bangus,* or boned stuffed milkfish, might be served. Milkfish is native to most areas of the Philippines. In addition, a wide assortment of desserts and pastries are placed on the Noche Buena table, such as bibingka, puto, and suman, each a form of rice cake; and *calamay,* which is toasted ground rice cooked in

coconut milk and sugar and then served in a coconut half shell. To some, calamay is a dessert that most represents Christmas. With their desserts, Filipinos of course enjoy hot salabat, or ginger tea. And fruit is always plentiful— mangoes, papayas, bananas, watermelons, pineapples, and guavas. Grapes and apples are a luxury, served usually by the more affluent. Some Filipinos save all year in order to purchase some of these more precious food items. It is important to serve the very best foods for Christmas.

The Noche Buena celebration is ongoing, much like an open

The Noche Buena *table awaits the hearty appetites of those who attended Midnight Mass.*

The Noche Buena *feast offers a variety of Filipino specialties. Surely, there is something for everyone.*

house. Neighbors drop by to wish the family "Maligayang Pasko!"—"Merry Christmas!" The streets are well lit and full of activity. The children run in and out—to play, to eat, to play again. The door is always open; people are always coming and going. Everyone is welcome.

Mostly the Christmas Eve gathering provides a reunion time for family members. Some families may choose to exchange gifts at this time; others wait until Christmas Day. But at the center of the family gathering is always a *Lola.* This is the endearing term used for a grandmother deeply respected, highly revered, always present. Some Filipinos remember

how their Lola had the children form a line and step up to receive a small gift of some coins. The older the child, the more coins he or she received. Often the youngsters would try to trick her by returning to the end of the line and stepping up again for a second gift. However, Lola was usually far too smart to fall for such a ploy. Others might remember a gift raffle of sorts that their Lola concocted for the grandchildren. She would hang numbers on the Christmas tree. After choosing a number, each child had to locate the Christmas package under the tree with the corresponding number. Still another Lola might gather the children in a circle and

Lola, *or Grandmother, passes the gifts around for her grandchildren.*

throw handfuls of coins in the air. Excitement filled the air as the children would scamper around the floor to fetch the coins. Such fond memories of a very special Lola.

Some families have a talent show during the Christmas Eve celebration. The children are asked to perform. Of course they know in advance that this may occur, so they are well prepared. One might sing a favorite Christmas carol or two, another might play a handmade musical instrument, or perhaps a few might do a dance. The adults love it and so do the children.

The celebration continues until 4, 5, even 6 o'clock in the morning. If the family is large and grown children with their families have come from distant barrios, sleeping mats are spread out on the floor. One group might lie down to catch a few minutes' rest. When they awake to rejoin the party, another group might take their place on the sleeping mats. Of course there are others who never go to sleep.

A few Filipino children do hang a stocking on Christmas Eve in hopes that Santa Claus will come and fill it with goodies. Some hang theirs on a bottom branch of the Christmas tree; others near the window. Most Filipino homes have no chimney for Santa to use, so the children must be assured that the door will be left unlatched. For the most part, however, these children know their gifts come from Mama and Papa.

Gift giving in the Philippines remains simple. In the provinces, gifts to friends or neighbors are often food items—produce, harvest items, or baked goods. Gifts of this nature are also sent to relatives in the city. Family members in the provinces look forward to receiving gifts purchased from the large department stores from their relatives in the city—perhaps a T-shirt or game for the children and a shirt or blouse for the adults. Money is often a welcome gift alternative. Even in the city, gifts are not very elaborate and are usually something practical. It is the quality tradition of sharing that is important to most Filipinos, not the quantity of the gifts. Often each family member receives just one gift—a dress or slippers for Mother, a shirt or robe for Father, a toy and some candy for the children.

As Christmas Day dawns and gifts are exchanged, those who did not attend Mass the night before will go to the morning Mass. Christmas morning breakfast might include *champorado*, a chocolate-flavored sweet rice

It is traditional for Filipino children to visit their godparents on Christmas Day. This child is showing respect for her godmother by touching her hand to her forehead. In return, she receives a gift.

porridge, often served with dried fish. More bibingka and other pastries along with salabat and tsokolate also appear on the breakfast table. Then it is a day for the children. They don their new Christmas clothes and go visiting, feeling very proud about how special they look.

Christmas Day is a popular day for visiting. The children make the rounds, accompanied by their parents, to see their godmothers, godfathers, aunts, uncles, and grandparents. At each home they are presented with a gift of some sort, usually candy, money, or a small toy. Christmas Day brings a constant stream of children to the homes of the family's elders—nieces, nephews, grandchildren, and godchildren all come to pay their respects. Food and treats are offered at each stop as well so that by the time the family arrives at the home where Christmas dinner will be hosted, they are already stuffed. But it is a day of family closeness; everyone wishes good cheer and glad tidings to all.

In the Philippines, godparents are especially respected and it is imperative that they be visited on Christmas Day. The children wish them Maligayang Pasko and kiss each one's hand to show respect, saying "Mano po, Ninong. Mano po, Ninang." "Let me kiss your hand, godfather. Let me kiss your hand, godmother." The children then take each benefactor's hand and touch it to their own forehead. In return the ninongs and ninangs usually present each godchild with their gift. Occasionally, the children perform for their godparents. They might sing, dance, or present a little play.

Most Filipino families get together around noon for the Christmas Day celebration with the family. The buffet table is refilled with some of the same delicacies that were served on Christmas Eve. A few additional entrees are put out as well. Small families might choose to have a sit-down dinner. But *lechon,* or roast suckling pig, is almost always the main Christmas entree. Most Filipinos don't feel their Christmas preparations are complete without lechon on the menu. It is generally the main course of choice at any important feast or celebration in the Philippines.

In the provinces, families raise a pig just for the purpose of Christmas dinner. It is slaughtered, cleaned and prepared, skewered on a bamboo pole, and placed over a charcoal pit on a large, homemade spit in the backyard. Grandfather or an uncle will fan the charcoal, turn the spit hour after hour, baste the pig with a secret blend of sauces, and watch the pig carefully all day long until it is cooked to perfection—the skin deliciously crisp and the meat meltingly tender. If one prefers, professional lechon makers can

Many Filipinos spend Christmas Day visiting with family. The children especially enjoy this chance to indulge in the tasty treats of the season.

be hired to come to the home with a live pig and tend to all the necessary preparations. Some members of the family like to make claims on their portion of the pig while it cooks. They must then be ready to take their chosen piece when the pig is carved.

Filipinos who live in big cities generally purchase a whole pig already roasted, at markets. The La Loma district of Quezon City is one of several famous lechon markets in Metro-Manila.

Dinner alternatives, for those families who cannot afford a whole pig or who have other preferences, might be the rellenong manok, stuffed chicken, or perhaps a Chinese ham. Desserts on Christmas would include the traditional bibingka and puto, but also the delicious

creamy caramel custard known as *leche flan.*

It is a joyous day for all Filipinos. Perhaps some families will pray together around the belen. Some may sing together their favorite Christmas carols. Most will hug and kiss and enjoy each other's company. And all will eat the wonderful foods they have saved all year to prepare and enjoy until they can barely look at another morsel. But every Filipino will end the day with a feeling of contentment, gratified in knowing they have shared Christmas Day with the family and friends who mean so much to them.

Light the Lantern

*I*f there is one symbol that most captures the essence and heart of the Filipino Christmas season it is the bamboo parol, or star lantern. To all Filipinos, the parol epitomizes the nature and spirit of Christmas. When every village home lights a Christmas lantern, a kind of revelation occurs. It is apparent that the entire community, the entire nation, shares the same spirit.

The roots of the parol can be found in the Mexican *piñata*. The piñata originated in Italy during the 1300's. It spread to Spain, then to Mexico, and finally to the Philippines. The Filipinos took the piñata and made changes to it. The inner pot of sweets was replaced with a candle. And the shape became that of a five-pointed star to represent the star of Bethlehem.

The star lantern has grown to magnificent proportions in some areas of the Philippines. One of the highlights of the Christmas season is the Christmas Eve lantern festival in San Fernando, the capital of

The San Fernando lantern festival, traditionally held on Christmas Eve, gives lantern makers a chance to show off their incredible talent.

Pampanga province, a town just an hour's drive from Manila. It is a spectacular fest of light and color. The festival's origins date back to the 1800's to Christmases in a Spanish Philippines. Its background is religious, being related to the nine pre-dawn Masses of Simbang Gabi. Back then prior to Mass, the Pampangos would parade down dirt roads through the barrios carrying colorful, candlelit lanterns made of bamboo and rice paper while singing religious hymns. Each of the nine days before Christmas would find different lanterns in the parade, ending with the finest and most impressive works of art displayed on Christmas Eve.

The festival orginated in Bacolor, the former capital of the province and San Fernando's next-door neighbor. But San Fernando, an up-and-coming city in the province, eventually became the home of the festival. It is the San Fernando parols that represent the ultimate in lantern art. The Pampango artisans are descendants of the original migrants from Indonesia, as well as Spanish Christians and wandering Chinese artisans who settled before and after the Spanish had settled there. The combination created a remarkable multidimensional heritage of superbly talented craftworkers.

Originally small, the lanterns were once carried to light the house-to-house caroling and the panunuluyan processions. But with the creativity and ingenuity of the Pampango artisan, the festival lanterns grew in intricacy and design to gargantuan proportions. The festival has become a technological wonder and the Pampango lantern makers are renowned nationwide, if not beyond.

Over the past six decades, the most common lantern shape, the five-pointed star, has evolved into a myriad of dazzling geometric shapes—the rose, the bromeliad, the snowflake, the sea urchin—each producing a kaleidoscopic effect of moving color. Each year festival designs and sizes seem to outdo those of the year before. Many of the lanterns can no longer be carried by hand, but must be mounted on flat-bed trucks. It's hard to imagine just how much grander the display may become.

Each lantern is a joint endeavor by residents of barrios throughout the province. In recent years, local businesses and government have begun sponsoring competitions for cash prizes. Each village combines its efforts, therefore, to produce a lantern of incredible design.

Over the years, the lantern designs have become much more complicated. For some, wire has replaced the wood or bamboo frame, welding has replaced old-fashioned glue, and electric light bulbs by the thousands have replaced the more romantic candles or

gaseras, the gas lamps that were once the norm. Professional electricians are often engaged to work on the complicated components that produce the dizzying light displays of the lanterns, each requiring its own generator and safety box. Often, the lantern frame is lined with gold or silver foil and then wrapped with cellophane crumpled just right to produce a textured effect. The traditional translucent colored rice paper is now used in combination with glossy Italian paper and pasted in layers to achieve pattern as well as tonal quality. Rotors within each lantern cause the 1,500 or more light bulbs to blink in time to the music of brass bands. Upon completion, the lanterns are transported by truck from surrounding Pampanga barrios and towns to the San Fernando plaza where they are paraded on Christmas Eve before Mass. Residents gather in the plaza to admire these marvelous moving swirls of color and light. These lanterns are truly an extraordinary labor of love.

Occasionally the San Fernando lantern festival is scheduled a day or two before Christmas Eve in order to accommodate the crowds that will view the magnificent display. In addition, the festival has become more than simply giant parols. Traditional Philippine games might be played at the center of town in the morning and a choral contest might take place in the afternoon. Food stalls are often set up around the San Fernando public market selling delicious Pampango delicacies—*tamales a la Pampanga;* peanut brittle; *longanisa,* or pork sausages; *tocino,* or cured sweet meat; and a wide variety of sweets and pastries made of cashew nuts, pounded rice, eggs, lemon, and refined sugar. It is truly a

The lanterns entered in the various lantern festivals throughout the Philippines have reached magnificent proportions—both in size and quality.

Star Lanterns: A Christmas Tradition

The star lanterns shown on these two pages are just a sampling of the diversity possible in creating these pieces of art.

Fun and games for the children are also a part of the lantern festivals and fiestas around Christmastime. Young boys are competing to reach the top of a greased bamboo pole (right). The first to finish eating his or her apple wins this contest (below).

fiesta beyond comparison to which visitors come from near and far.

Lantern competitions are held in many cities throughout the Philippines just before Christmas, though not nearly as elaborate as the San Fernando festival. A single community might have its own competition with judges awarding a prize to the best individual entry. The lanterns might be paraded through the streets of the village to a public stage or church square where the awards are presented. And schoolchildren enjoy parades and lantern competitions in schools before the Christmas holidays.

Parol making has become a seasonal cottage industry in the Philippines. Stalls with lanterns for sale appear everywhere just before Christmas. An entire stretch of the national highway near the town of Gerona in Tarlac province welcomes travelers with a multitude of such stalls. And the thoroughfare in Las Piñas, Metro-Manila, is famous for its array of lantern stalls. However, the best bargains on lanterns in Manila can be found at the Central Market, Divisoria, or the Quinta Market under the Quezon Bridge.

Parols are on display everywhere during the Philippine Christmas season. In the town of Imus in Cavite province, a large lantern is hung on every street corner, often including a diorama of the Nativity. A brightly colored lantern can be seen hanging from every lamppost covering a long stretch of Roxas Boulevard and other Manila streets and avenues. Rizal Park in Manila usually has a magnificent lantern display, often including some of the winning entries from the San Fernando lantern festival. And at the Araneta Commercial Center in Quezon City, a huge Christmas tree is fashioned out of a bevy of interlinked star-shaped lanterns.

The parol truly brightens the Christmas holidays throughout the Philippines. It scatters the warmth and spirit shared by all Filipinos to every corner of the nation. From the extravagant lanterns of the San Fernando festival to the small, candlelit, home-grown variety, each tugs at the heartstrings of every Filipino. It is almost impossible for most to disassociate Christmas from the star lantern. It is the star of Bethlehem and its Philippine symbol, the parol, that will shine always in the hearts of all Filipinos.

The Star

I do not think the three Wise Men
Were Persian Kings at all.
I think it much more likely they
Set sail from out Manila Bay
In answer to the call.

And though the great historians
May stare at me, and frown
I still maintain the three Wise Men
Were kings from my home town.

And if you ask why I affirm
That Melchior was King of Tonado,
When Gaspar ruled Sampaloc,
And Balthazar Binondo—
We will not argue. We will walk
The streets on Christmas Eve,
And I will show you the poor man's
    rafter,
Where hangs the Star the Kings
    sought after,
High above Christian prayer and
    laughter—
You will see it, and believe!

For when they crossed the sea again
From Bethlehem afar,
They lost their camels in the sea,
And they forgot the Christmas tree,
But they brought back to you and me
The secret of the Star.

Father Horacio de la Costa

"The Star" from *Fiesta* by Alejandra R. Roces.
Copyright 1980 by Vera-Reyes, Inc.
Reprinted with permission.

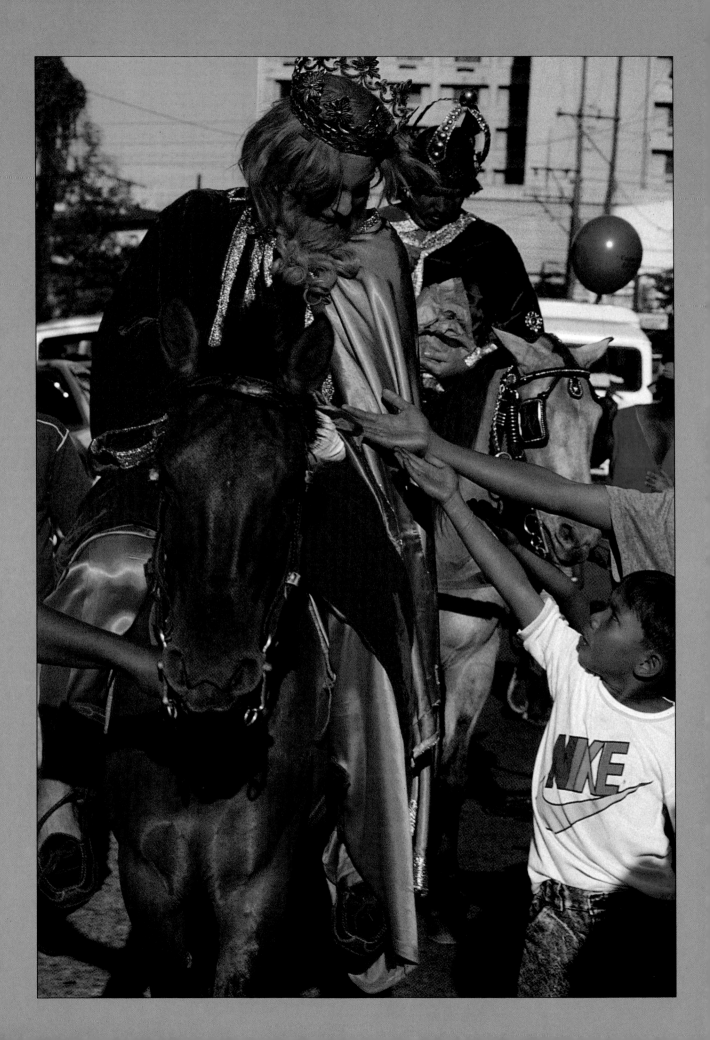

The Twelve Days of Christmas

The Christmas season in the Philippines extends twelve days beyond Christmas Day. The official end of the season is marked by Three Kings Day on January 6. Filipinos try before Three Kings Day to visit those family members or friends they may not have seen earlier.

The holiday atmosphere and air of celebration continues throughout the entire season. There are parties, continual cooking and baking, and gatherings galore. But beyond the usual get-togethers of families and friends, there are numerous holiday events taking place in cities and towns all across the country. Beginning very early in December, lists of concerts and holiday programs appear in local newspapers. Calendars are filled with holiday activities the whole season long. Large cities in particular have much to offer fun-loving Filipinos. There is holiday entertainment to fit every age and every taste.

Three Kings Day, celebrated on the first Sunday after New Year's Day, marks the end of the Christmas season. Many communities hold a parade for the occasion. This parade is on Roxas Boulevard in Manila's tourist district. The kings ride horseback and distribute gifts to children and the needy.

The nation's parks are especially full of activity during Christmas. Rizal Park in Manila usually features a large parol competition and display as well as the traditional Simbang Gabi Masses held for churchgoers in the park's open theater. Philippine actors and actresses often return the patronage of their faithful fans by making free appearances in Rizal Park during the holiday season. On each of the four Sundays in December, Rizal Park also holds its annual Concert in the Park series featuring such musical groups as the Manila Symphony Orchestra, the internationally renowned University of the Philippines Concert Chorus, and the University of the Philippines Singing Ambassadors. Similarly, Friday evenings in December also find Paco Park, in the Paco district of Manila, filled with citizens looking for holiday entertainment. Perhaps they'll hear the Cultural Center of the Philippines French Horn Quintet, the University of the Philippines Madrigal Singers Alumni, or the Philharmonic Strings Ensemble in the charming setting that this circular public park offers.

Fiesta Intramuros is a month-long fiesta in December that takes place within the old walled city. It focuses on the rich cultural, historical, and

Because of the warm weather in the Philippines, much of the holiday celebration takes place outdoors. Here, people attend Simbang Gabi *on the grounds of the Folk Arts Theater in Manila.*

religious heritage of Intramuros. It begins with the famous Marian procession in honor of the Feast of the Immaculate Conception, which is December 8. The procession is a parade of images of the Virgin Mary from all over the Philippines. It starts at San Agustin Church in Intramuros and proceeds to the Quirino Grandstand in Rizal Park. The fiesta also includes the Puerta Real Evenings, a series of free Saturday evening cultural performances held at Puerta Real in Intramuros featuring such presentations as a holiday ballet, a performance of *Amahl and the Night Visitors,* or the Philippine Army Band playing Christmas carols.

Casa Manila in Intramuros is also the scene of much holiday activity. Casa Manila is a carefully restored "living museum" reflecting life of the well-to-do in Intramuros at the turn of the century. Here, throughout the month of December, there might be free puppet shows for the children, competitions of school and church choirs singing beautiful Spanish and Pilipino carols, a toy sale and demonstration, or an exhibit of *santos,* statues of saints, whose feast days fall in the month of December.

The Metropolitan Theater in Manila, fondly dubbed the MET, is another favorite spot for many Filipinos at Christmastime. The MET is home to the Manila Symphony Orchestra, which frequently presents holiday concerts here. And the MET

Street vendors, expecting a lot of business, arrange the New Year's hats they have for sale.

inches (12.5 centimeters) in diameter. It was recently sent to Germany for a complete over-haul and now plays out holiday carols to perfection.

And at the Greenhills Commercial Complex and Shopping Center in San Juan, Metro-Manila, Filipinos can gaze in awe and wonder at a miniature belen that has been constructed on a stage area 48 feet (14.5 meters) long by 30 feet (9 meters) deep and 10 feet (3 meters) high. The tableau's landscape and buildings are made with over 30 large bags of plaster of Paris and the scene supports a cast of more than 200 figurines. Hundreds of tiny light bulbs simulate fires, the moon, and the stars. Water is pumped across the landscape as a small river. It is truly an amazing effort. As visitors take time to pore over the textured landscape of this remarkable belen, they are surely reminded of the true meaning of Christmas.

Planned for late 1990 is the opening of the Philippine Christmas Village in San Fernando, Pampanga—home of the Christmas Eve Lantern Festival. The village will be the third of its kind in the world. With plans to be open year-round, the village will showcase Filipino culture with a Christmas theme. Features will include typical Christmas displays and fiesta activities, a sample Filipino home, handicraft demonstrations, gift shops, museums, an amphitheater, an art gallery,

Chorus and Dance Theater often combine with local actors in staging Christmas musical presentations.

Another special treat at Christmastime is to hear the famous bamboo organ at San Jose Church in Las Piñas, Metro-Manila. The unique organ is more than 150 years old and has about 800 bamboo pipes, the longest of which is 8 feet (2.4 meters) long and 5

restaurants, and much more. The village will have the shape of a Christmas star lantern.

Thus, holiday amusements and diversions abound in the Philippines. Filipinos know they need only peruse the entertainment pages of the local newspaper any day of the season to find something suitable to their tastes and desires. There is truly something for everyone.

As the season continues, the two days following December 25 are usually relatively quiet days of rest, with perhaps some visiting attended to. Then arrives December 28, Holy Innocents' Day. This day commemorates Herod's massacre of all children in Bethlehem under 2 years old, when he tried to kill Jesus. But contrary to the frightfulness of the story, Holy Innocents' Day in the Philippines is a frolicking day of fun. On this day, many Filipinos enjoy playing a variety of pranks. The rule is, if you are successful in putting something over on a friend or colleague, you are absolved of all wrongdoing; if you manage to borrow money from a friend or relative,

Deciding which hat to wear to bring in the new year is not easy for this young child.

you need not pay it back. Most Filipinos are wary and refuse to lend anything on this day. But woe to him or her who forgets what day it is! This custom is especially fun among office-mates. If one succeeds in borrowing money from a fellow worker, he or she might use it to buy some good things to eat and share with the entire staff. Everyone has a big laugh.

The island of Marinduque celebrates December 28, *Niños Inocentes,* with a festival featuring people in masks and costumed as giants and dwarfs. They parade through the streets mimicking Herod's soldiers in search of the infant Jesus.

After the Christmas parties and celebrations are over, Filipinos everywhere begin anticipating the riotous New Year festivities. Incredible noise and abundant merrymaking are the rule on this holiday. It is a hectic and rowdy celebration. Starting early on December 31, sounds of exploding firecrackers fill the air. Although it is illegal to purchase fireworks in the Philippines, they are easily bought from hawkers and vendors in sidewalk stalls throughout the holiday season. Some

Filipinos set up a homemade fireworks display in their backyard. Others may choose to beat drums, pans, or empty cans. Some might even tie a string of empty tin cans to their cars and cruise around the neighborhood. All this noise-making has its origins in the folk belief that the noisier the celebration, the more prosperous the New Year will be.

Later on New Year's Eve, sidewalks and businesses come alive with festive party hats and raucous noisemakers, which eager merchants try out to entice shoppers to buy. Many city dwellers ring in the New Year at nightclubs or New Year's balls. Others gather with family and friends for a *media noche,* a midnight repast, in the quiet of their own homes. In rural areas, gatherings are simple and family oriented. Public fireworks displays are common and well attended. In Manila, there is an extravagant fireworks exhibition staged on New Year's Eve in Rizal Park. The fireworks are launched from barges in Manila Bay, which itself provides a reflection pool of sorts for the spectacular light show.

At midnight, church bells ring, sirens blow, radios blare, and boats in the harbor sound their whistles. Families might venture into the street and toast the New Year with neighbors. Many feel it is important to pay their respects to village elders and wish them "Manigong Bagong Taon!"—"Happy New Year!"—or "Masaganang Bagong Taon!"—"Prosperous New Year!" Many Filipinos attend midnight Mass on New Year's Eve. If not, they will go to church on New Year's Day.

When the frenzy dies down, everyone is ready to head for the sumptuous New Year's Eve media noche table. Food is an important part of the New Year's celebration, a sign of hope for prosperity to come. Ham, the stuffed pepper called *relleno,* fruits of the season, and all the typical pastries and sweet delicacies are served. Grapes in particular, if affordable, are an important food item for the New Year's feast. They are a sign of abundance. Some even believe that eating 12 grapes in succession as midnight arrives will provide good luck in the coming year.

All things round seem to be a New Year's symbol of good luck or prosperity in the Philippines. Many people insist on wearing polka-dotted clothing on New Year's Eve. Women might plan well ahead to have a dress with a circular or polka-dotted design for the celebration. Many are sure to jingle a pocketful of coins all evening long. And it is important to stock up on food staples for the year, especially "round" eggs, vegetables, or fruits, so that food will be abundant in the new year.

Other superstitions include turning on all the house lights at midnight to ensure that the rest of the year will be bright. Many believe in making their New Year's resolutions as the church bells peal and whistles blow at midnight. They are certain these wishes will come true. Some families in rural areas have fun listening for animal noises at the stroke of midnight. They believe that the first animal sound they hear will determine the state of their lives for the coming year. There is, of course, an interpretation for each animal. Should Uncle Achilles hear a cow, because it eats grass, he will probably have abundance. But poor Aunt Prudenciana if she hears a chicken! Because it scratches for its food, she may spend the year scratching out an existence.

Many Filipinos feel they should remain in their own homes on the first day of the year or else the new year will find them always away from their families. Similarly, many feel that the entire year is influenced by what happens on the first day. If January 1 is sunny, the whole year will be sunny; if it is dreary on the first day, it will be a dreary year. And some Filipinos try hard to go as long as possible on the first day of the new year without spending, lest they be without money the whole year through.

Everyone wears their new holiday clothes and shoes on New Year's Day. All must be at their best for church or for visiting family and friends. The house, too, is spotless for family that may drop in to say "Manigong Bagong Taon!" And food must always be plentiful in case visitors should stop by on this holiday or the remaining days of the season.

After a few days' breathing space, the final festival of the holiday season approaches—the Feast of the Three Kings on January 6. For the sake of celebration, the holiday has become a movable feast and is now celebrated on the first Sunday of January. The day generally begins for most Filipinos with attendance at Mass. Often there will be a small dramatization in the church of the Three Kings' search for the Christ child. A procession with costumed, gift-bearing kings or with statues of the kings will accompany the priest down the aisle prior to Mass. Later in the day there are gatherings with family and friends. For the most part, it is a day for the children. Small gifts are given by family and friends to the children—candies, coins, or small trinkets or toys. Some children place their shoes, well-shined of course, near the window on the eve of Three Kings Day. The hope is that the camels of the Three Kings will pass by the window and the kings will drop gifts in their shoes. First thing in the morning, the children scurry outside to look for

Children enjoy celebrating New Year's Eve because it gives them the chance to make a lot of noise.

camel tracks beneath the window.

Charitable institutions often save this day for charity work. Community members might pose as the Three Kings and distribute gifts to children in orphanages, hospitals, or less-privileged families. Occasionally private clubs stage pageants where three costumed kings appear and present gifts to the children of club members.

In many communities throughout the Philippines colorful parades and processions with costumed kings on horseback are held reenacting the coming of the Magi. The towns of Santa Cruz and Gasan in the island province of Marinduque

Three Kings Day is a children's holiday in the Philippines. Here, some lucky youngsters ride in the parade with the Magi.

stage a festival resplendent with pageantry on this feast day. Street players dressed as the Three Kings in full regalia ride through the town on horseback followed closely by their entourage—villagers in native costumes, masked characters, bamboo musicians, and giant puppets. The assemblage grows as ecstatic children join the procession. As spectators throw bags of candies and coins, the youngsters shriek with joy. The event culminates with a pantomime of Herod, full of rage, destroying his own palace after learning of the Christ child's birth.

So ends the Philippine Christmas season. The celebrating is over, the precious parols are packed away, life returns to normal. Many Filipinos are grateful to return to everyday activities. Most feel exhausted, though happy and full—of joy, spirit, and good will. These feelings linger in the Philippines for quite some time. Those little star lanterns will stay lit in the hearts of all Filipinos for a long while, indeed until next Christmas.

Make a Star Lantern

The star lantern is an essential Christmas decoration in the Philippines. Many Filipino families make their own lanterns. Follow the directions on the next few pages and you too can make your own star lantern.

Materials

10 strips of balsa wood, 1/4 inch wide, 10 inches long (or strips made from matte board, 1/4 inch wide, 10 inches long)

5 strips of balsa wood, 1/4 inch wide, 3/4 inch long (or strips made from matte board, 1/4 inch wide, 3/4 inch long)

2 12-inch squares of tissue paper, white or colored

2 8-inch by 16-inch pieces of tissue paper, white or colored

5 10-inch by 3-inch pieces of tissue paper, white or colored

2 pieces of thin, flexible wire, cut into 6-inch lengths

1 piece of thin, flexible wire, cut into a 10-inch length

construction paper
foil
non-toxic glue
tape
pencil
ruler
scissors
markers
glitter
compass

1. Using the star pattern shown here (pattern 1) as a guide, glue five of the 10-inch strips of wood or matte board to make a star. Allow the glue to dry completely. Repeat with the other five strips. The two stars should be identical.

2. At the five joints of one of the stars, glue the five 3/4-inch strips of wood or matte board so they are in an upright position (figure A). Allow the glue to dry.

3. Place a dab of glue on the top of each of the shorter strips. Position the second star directly over the first one (figure B). Apply a bit of pressure at the joints to be sure they affix to the shorter strips.

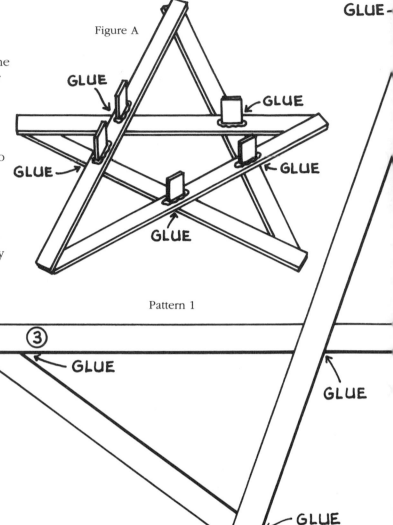

Figure A

GLUE

GLUE

GLUE

GLUE

GLUE

GLUE

Pattern 1

③

GLUE

GLUE

GLUE

⑤

GLUE

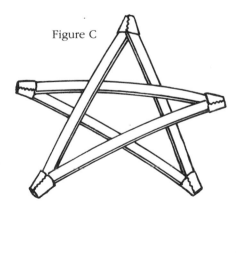

Figure B

4. To finish joining the stars, place a dab of glue at the five points of the first star. Press together the points of the two stars. Use tape to secure the points until the glue dries (figure C); then, remove the tape. Be careful not to pull the points apart.

Figure C

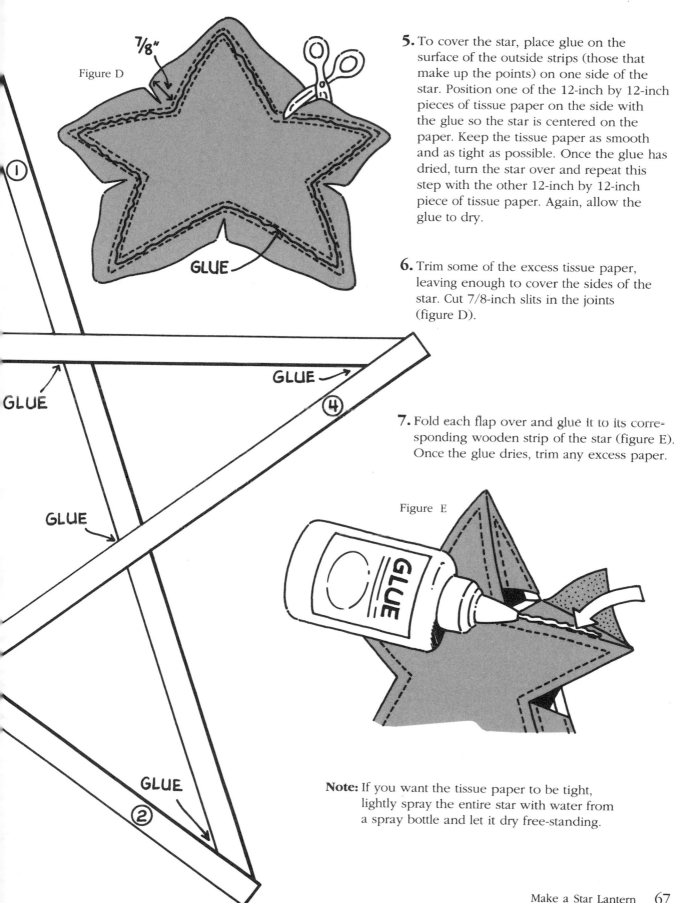

Figure D

7/8"

GLUE

GLUE

GLUE

GLUE

GLUE

GLUE

5. To cover the star, place glue on the surface of the outside strips (those that make up the points) on one side of the star. Position one of the 12-inch by 12-inch pieces of tissue paper on the side with the glue so the star is centered on the paper. Keep the tissue paper as smooth and as tight as possible. Once the glue has dried, turn the star over and repeat this step with the other 12-inch by 12-inch piece of tissue paper. Again, allow the glue to dry.

6. Trim some of the excess tissue paper, leaving enough to cover the sides of the star. Cut 7/8-inch slits in the joints (figure D).

7. Fold each flap over and glue it to its corresponding wooden strip of the star (figure E). Once the glue dries, trim any excess paper.

Figure E

GLUE

Note: If you want the tissue paper to be tight, lightly spray the entire star with water from a spray bottle and let it dry free-standing.

8. While the star is drying, make the paper tassels. These look best if a different color tissue paper from that which covers the star is used. Fold each of the two 8-inch by 16-inch pieces of tissue paper so the 16-inch length is in half. With the scissors, make cuts 3/8 inch wide and 6 inches long, leaving 2 inches at the folded side (figure F).

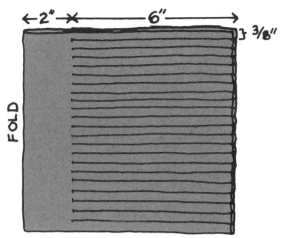

Figure F

9. Open one of the tassels so there is fringe at both ends. Fold the tassel in half lengthwise, and squeeze both sides of the center (figure G). Poke one half of a 6-inch wire through the center of the tassel. Repeat these steps with the other tassel.

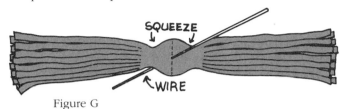

Figure G

10. Fold the tassel in half so all the fringe is together. Wrap the bottom half of the wire (that which is now covered with the fringe) around the area just at the top of the fringe (figure H). Repeat with the other tassel using the second 6-inch wire.

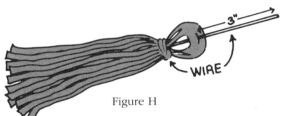

Figure H

11. Attach the tassels to the lower points of the star by poking the 3 inches of exposed wire through the tissue paper on the star. Wrap the wire around the point of the star.

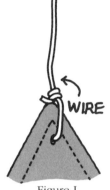

Figure I

12. Poke 2 inches of the 10-inch wire through the tissue paper at the top point of the star. Wrap the 2 inches of wire around the point and wrap the end around the remaining wire (figure I). Use the 8 inches of wire left over to form a hanger.

13. To cover the wires of the tassels at the bottom points and to put tassels on the other three points, fold in half each of the five 10-inch pieces of tissue paper. With the scissors, make cuts 1/8 inch wide and 2 1/2 inches long, leaving 1/2 inch at the top (figure J).

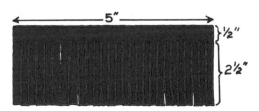

Figure J

14. To attach the tassels, spread glue on the uncut 1/2-inch area. Carefully wind the glued end around each of the five points of the star (figure K).

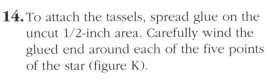

Figure K

15. Many things can be done to further decorate the star. Spread glue on the star and cover with glitter. Use markers to draw pictures on the star. Cut a small star out of foil and place it in the center of the star lantern.

FOLD

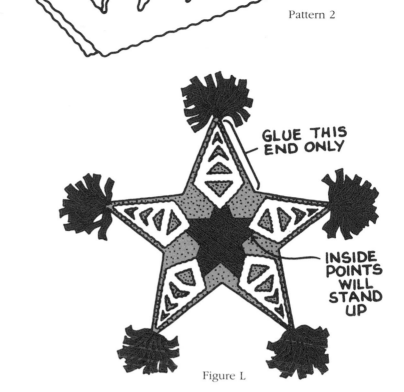

Pattern 2

GLUE THIS END ONLY

INSIDE POINTS WILL STAND UP

Figure L

16. Cut patterns out of construction paper and glue them on the star. Make up a pattern or use the pattern shown (pattern 2). To do so, fold a sheet of construction paper in half. Copy the pattern onto the paper, making sure the fold on the paper corresponds with the fold on the pattern, and then cut the pattern out. Use a zig zag motion with the scissors to create a unique edge. Unfold the paper and place glue only on the longer edges. Position the pattern on the star with the glued end toward the tassel (figure L). Repeat this step with the other four points of the star.

17. Paper scallops can be glued to the sides of the star. With a compass, draw a 4 1/2-inch circle on construction paper. Cut the circle out, fold in half, and cut along the fold line. Fold the half circle in half four more times until you get a very small wedge (figure M).

Figure M

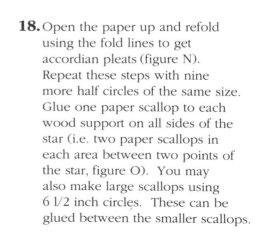

Figure N

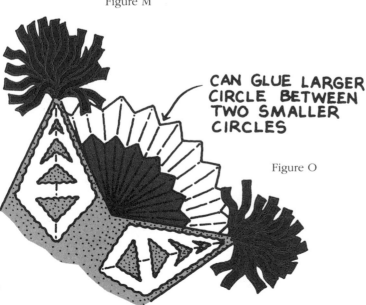

CAN GLUE LARGER CIRCLE BETWEEN TWO SMALLER CIRCLES

Figure O

18. Open the paper up and refold using the fold lines to get accordian pleats (figure N). Repeat these steps with nine more half circles of the same size. Glue one paper scallop to each wood support on all sides of the star (i.e. two paper scallops in each area between two points of the star, figure O). You may also make large scallops using 6 1/2 inch circles. These can be glued between the smaller scallops.

Create a Holiday Feast

Ukoy—Shrimp Snacks

1 c. plus 2 tbsp. all-purpose flour
2 t. baking powder
3/4 t. salt
2 eggs, slightly beaten
1/2 c. water
1/2 t. white pepper
1 clove garlic, crushed
1/3 c. finely chopped green onions
1 c. cooked baby shrimp, chopped
vegetable oil
vinegar
soy sauce

Combine flour, baking powder, and salt in a medium bowl. Add eggs, water, pepper, garlic, and green onions. Mix until smooth. Stir in shrimp. Heat oil in medium saucepan to 375°F. Drop batter by tablespoonfuls into hot oil. Cook until golden brown 3 to 4 minutes. Drain. Serve with dips of vinegar and soy sauce.
Makes 22 to 24 snacks

Lumpia Sauce*

2 tbsp. cornstarch
1/4 c. light brown sugar
1/2 c. water
1/2 c. pineapple juice
1/4 c. soy sauce
2 tbsp. vinegar mixed with 2 tbsp. water
1 t. oil
2 cloves garlic, minced

Combine cornstarch and brown sugar in small saucepan. Stir in water, pineapple juice, soy sauce, and vinegar-water mixture. Heat to boiling. Boil 2 minutes to thicken. Meanwhile, heat oil in small skillet. Sauté garlic in oil 2 to 3 minutes. Add sauce to mixture.

*To be served with Lumpia from recipe card.

Chicken-Rice Soup

3 tbsp. vegetable oil
2 tbsp. minced garlic
1/4 c. chopped onion
8 1/2-inch slices fresh ginger
2 to 31/2-lb. chicken, cut into small serving pieces
6 c. water
2 c. uncooked rice
2 t. salt
1/4 c. chopped green onions
1/4 t. freshly ground pepper

Heat oil in a 5-quart Dutch oven. Sauté garlic, onion, and ginger until tender, 2 to 3 minutes. Add the chicken pieces and brown lightly. Cover and let simmer 5 minutes. Add water, rice, and salt. Heat to boiling. Cover and simmer until chicken and rice are tender. Add chopped green onions and pepper before serving.
Makes 6 to 8 servings

Pan-Fried Roast Pork*

2- to 3-lb. pork shoulder, with skin
4 c. water
2 tbsp. salt
1 to 2 c. cooking oil
2 c. liver sauce (see recipe card for
    Roast Suckling Pig)

Boil pork in water with salt until skin is tender. Remove from heat and drain.

Cool and air dry. Deep-fry in oil until tiny blisters appear on the skin. Chop into serving pieces. Serve with liver sauce or a dip of vinegar, salt, and crushed garlic.
Makes 4 servings

*This may be served as an alternative to Roast Suckling Pig.

Kare-Kare— Oxtail Stew in Peanut Butter Sauce

3 lb. oxtail, cut into serving pieces
6 c. water
2 tbsp. finely minced garlic
1 c. chopped onion
4 tbsp. cooking oil
1/2 c. anatto water*
1/2 c. raw rice, ground to a powder in
    a food processor or blender and
    roasted in a pan at 350°F until brown
1 c. peanut butter
1 lb. eggplant, coarsely chopped
10 string beans, cut into 2-inch lengths
1 small cabbage, quartered
salt and freshly ground pepper to taste

Boil oxtail in water for an hour or until tender. Set stock aside. Sauté garlic and onion in oil in a large saucepan. Add anatto water and oxtail to saucepan and bring to a boil. Stir in roast rice powder and peanut butter. Add four cups reserved stock, eggplant, string beans, and cabbage and mix well. Bring to a boil and simmer for 10 minutes. Season with salt and pepper to taste.
Makes 6 to 8 servings

*Anatto water is available bottled in Oriental markets. If liquid is not available, purchase anatto seeds and crush 1 tablespoon in 1/2 cup water. Let stand 30 minutes. Strain water and discard the seeds.

From *The Philippine Cookbook* by Reynaldo Alejandro. Copyright ©1982 by Photographic Book Company, Inc. Reprinted by permission of The Putnam Publishing Group and the Photographic Book Company.

Meat Turnovers

1 lb. ground beef
1 clove garlic, minced
1 small onion, chopped
1 c. diced, cooked potatoes
1 t. salt
1/4 t. pepper
1/2 c. seedless raisins

Pastry
3 c. all-purpose flour
1/4 c. sugar
1/2 t. salt
1/2 c. water
1/3 c. oil
3 egg yolks (plus some egg whites for
    sealing the turnovers)

Brown ground beef. Push meat to one side and sauté garlic until brown, then add onion. Mix the meat, garlic, onion, and potatoes. Stir and cook 2 to 3 minutes longer. Season with salt and pepper and mix in raisins. Set aside.

Mix and knead all pastry ingredients, except egg whites, until dough is soft. On a floured board, roll dough out 1/8-inch thick. Cut into 4- or 5-inch circles (use a wide mouth cup or jar for cutting circles). Put a spoonful of meat filling in center of each circle. Fold to half-moon shape, wet edges with egg white, press and seal sides. Deep-fry until golden brown and drain. Or, instead of deep-frying, turnovers can be baked in preheated 425°F oven for 15 to 20 minutes or until golden brown.
Makes 20 turnovers

From *The Philippine Cookbook* by Reynaldo Alejandro. Copyright © 1982 by Photographic Book Company, Inc. Reprinted by permission of The Putnam Publishing Group and the Photographic Book Company.

Rellenong Manok— Baked Stuffed Chicken

1 whole 3 1/2- to 4-lb. chicken, boned
3 tbsp. soy sauce
1 tbsp. sugar
2 tbsp. lemon juice

Stuffing
1/2 lb. ground ham
1/2 lb. ground pork
1/2 lb. ground chicken
1/4 lb. frankfurters, finely chopped
2 tbsp. raisins
1 tbsp. lemon juice
2 tbsp. soy sauce
1 tbsp. garlic powder
2 tbsp. breadcrumbs
1/4 c. chopped onion
1/3 c. sweet pickle relish
2 eggs
2 t. pepper
salt to taste
3 hard-boiled eggs, peeled
1/2 c. melted butter or margarine
2 pieces (about 8 oz.) spicy sausage,
    sliced lengthwise into quarters

Sauce
drippings from chicken
2 tbsp. flour
2 tbsp. soy sauce
1 tbsp. finely minced garlic
2 tbsp. vegetable or corn oil
salt to taste

Combine 3 tbsp. soy sauce, 1 tbsp. sugar, and 2 tbsp. lemon juice. Marinate boned chicken for three hours in the mixture.

Combine all the ingredients for stuffing except the hard-boiled eggs, melted butter or margarine, and sausage. Mix well. Stuff the chicken with the mixture and the 3 hard-boiled eggs and sausage, taking care to arrange the eggs and sausage inside the chicken from neck to tail. Sew the slits at the neck and tail. Place chicken in a baking dish and brush with melted butter or margarine. Wrap in aluminum foil. Preheat oven to 350°F. Bake chicken for 1 hour. Remove aluminum-foil wrapper and continue baking until chicken is golden brown.

For sauce, collect drippings from the baking dish. Add flour and 2 tbsp. soy sauce. Set aside. In a small saucepan, sauté garlic in oil until brown. Add the mixture of flour, soy sauce, and drippings. Season with salt. Cook about 15 minutes, stirring often. Slice chicken and serve with sauce.
Makes 8 servings

From *The Philippine Cookbook* by Reynaldo Alejandro. Copyright © 1982 by Photographic Book Company, Inc. Reprinted by permission of The Putnam Publishing Group and the Photographic Book Company.

Banana Fritters

vegetable oil
1 c. flour
1 t. baking powder
2 tbsp. sugar
1/2 t. salt
4 tbsp. milk
1/3 c. water
1 egg, beaten
8 bananas
granulated sugar

Pour oil in a skillet or electric frypan to a depth of 2 inches. Heat to 375°F.

Sift together the flour, baking powder, sugar, and salt. Set aside. Mix together milk, water, and egg. Add this mixture to the sifted ingredients. Mix well until smooth. Set aside.

Peel bananas and slice lengthwise. Roll in flour and dip in batter until the batter is evenly distributed on the bananas. Fry the batter-dipped bananas in hot oil until brown. Drain and coat with sugar before serving.
Makes 8 fritters

From *The Philippine Cookbook* by Reynaldo Alejandro. Copyright © 1982 by Photographic Book Company, Inc. Reprinted by permission of The Putnam Publishing Group and the Photographic Book Company.

Churros— Crullers

vegetable oil
2¼ c. all-purpose flour
1 tbsp. baking powder
1/2 t. salt
2 eggs
2/3 c. sugar
3/4 c. milk
2 tbsp. butter, melted
1/2 t. vanilla
confectioner's sugar

Pour oil in a skillet or electric frypan to a depth of 2 inches. Heat to 375°F.

Mix flour, baking powder, and salt.

In a separate bowl, beat eggs and sugar until thick and lemon-colored. Beat in flour mixture alternately with milk. Stir in butter and vanilla.

Fit a pastry tube with a large star tip. Fill with dough. Squeeze dough carefully into hot oil in 6-inch lengths, cutting off end with a knife. Fry until golden brown, about 1½ minutes on each side. Drain on paper towels. Sprinkle with confectioner's sugar and serve warm.
Makes about 30 crullers

Salabat— Ginger Tea

1/2 lb. fresh, sliced ginger
5 c. water
1 c. brown sugar

Boil all ingredients together in a saucepan for 30 minutes or longer, depending on strength of tea desired. Add more water if tea is too strong. Strain and serve hot.
Makes about 4 servings

From *The Philippine Cookbook* by Reynaldo Alejandro. Copyright © 1982 by Photographic Book Company, Inc. Reprinted by permission of The Putnam Publishing Group and the Photographic Book Company.

Tsokolate

6 c. milk
3 c. (18 oz.) semi-sweet chocolate chips
6 egg yolks

Heat milk until hot in a large saucepan. Stir in chocolate pieces and heat over low until chocolate has melted. Beat egg yolks slightly. Whisk into hot milk mixture and beat over low heat until frothy, 2 to 3 minutes.
Makes 4 to 6 servings

Rejoice With Music

Philippine Carol

Words by LEVI CELERIO
Translated by
JOHN MORRISON

LEVI CELERIO
arr. W. L. REED

(Ang Pasko
ay sumapit)

O mer-ry Christ-mas sea - son, Ring it out on loud ca-

ril - lon, O mer-ry Christ-mas sea - son, Come and e -ver with us

stay! And let ev-'ry-one, re-joic-ing, In a grate-ful ca-rol voic - ing

*The bottom G sharps may be omitted

O Naggasat Ketdin Daytoy Nga Rabii

(Oh, How Blessed
Is This Night)

Music and Lyrics:
REALITO H. INAY

Bit-bi-tuen diay nga-to i-pa-ra nga-rang-da ____

An ge-les diay la-ngit ket ka-kan ta-an-da ____

Ti na-tan-ok a-na-gan ken ti da-yag-na ____

Danggayan met a-weng tun-tu-no 'dtoy ____ da-ga. ____

Pus-pu-so ken biag tay nga-rud i-sa-ga nan ____

Oh, how blessed is this night
That the King we were hoping
To save and bring peace to the world
From heaven now to us descended.

Stars in the sky are proclaiming
Angels in heavens are singing
With joining earth melodies are sounding
All to His great name and glory.

So let's prepare our life and hearts
And go and bow down and praise
Jesus the King and Savior
In the town where he was born.

Dimtengen Kadatay

(Now He Is Here)

Music and Lyrics:
JONATHAN GALLO

'Twas only a stable
Where He was born
The King of the universe
Has come to save men.

'Twas only a stable
Where He was laid
This child called Jesus
King of the universe.

Refrain:
The King has come to
dwell in this world
He has come to this
world to save us.

Acknowledgements

Cover: © Goloyugo, Prime Inc.

2: © Ortega, Prime Inc.

6: © Santiago, Prime Inc.

9: © Cabrera, Prime Inc

10: © Santiago, Prime Inc.

12: © Santiago, Prime Inc.

13: © Cabrera, Prime Inc.

15: © Cabrera, Prime Inc.

16: © Peralta, Prime Inc.

19: Philippines Department of Tourism

20: Philippines Department of Tourism

21: Philippines Department of Tourism

22: © Santiago, Prime Inc.

24: © NET, Prime Inc.

25: © Peralta, Prime Inc.

27: Philippines Department of Tourism

28: © Cabrera, Prime Inc.

31: © Sakdalan, Prime Inc.

32: © Baluyot, Prime Inc.

34: © Sakdalan, Prime Inc.

35: © Baluyot, Prime Inc.

36: © Cabrera, Prime Inc.

37: © Baluyot, Prime Inc.

39: Philippines Department of Tourism

40: © Santiago, Prime Inc.

41: © Ortega, Prime Inc.

42: © Ortega, Prime Inc.

43: © Santiago, Prime Inc.

45: © Santiago, Prime Inc.

46: © Santiago, Prime Inc.

49: © Cabrera, Prime Inc.

50: (Top) Philippines Department of Tourism
(Bottom) Philippines Department of Tourism

51: (Top) © Santiago, Prime Inc.
(Bottom) © Cabrera, Prime Inc.

52: (Top) © Ortega, Prime Inc.
(Bottom) © Cabrera, Prime Inc.

54: © Santiago, Prime Inc.

56: © NET, Prime Inc.

57: © Cabrera, Prime Inc.

58: © Santiago, Prime Inc.

59: © Sakdalan, Prime Inc.

60: © Philippines Department of Tourism

63: © Santiago, Prime Inc.

64: © Santiago, Prime Inc.